From
These
Roots
& Other Poems

Thomas Amherst Perry

FROM
THESE
ROOTS
& OTHER POEMS
THOMAS AMHERST PERRY

Pentland Press, Inc.
England • USA • Scotland

PUBLISHED BY PENTLAND PRESS, INC.
5124 Bur Oak Circle, Raleigh, North Carolina 27612
United States of America
919-782-0281

Assistance on cover design graciously provided by Charles E. McGough.

ISBN 1-57197-027-4
Library of Congress Catalog Card Number 96-68830

Printed in the United States of America

With love to my wife
Lora Margaret

FOREWORD

These poems are about some of the events and issues of most con-
cern today. There is the growing and enervating dependence upon the
state; my concern about this has been deepened by my experiences abroad,
especially in East Europe. There is the threat to our cultural heritage in a
Modernism that would cut our ties to our roots, roots needed for wisdom,
emotional sustenance, and direction. There are within each race ethnic
chauvinists, isolationists, hostile to all others, who distort this heritage into
a racist fetish. There are individuals of mixed race, who, uncertain of their
roots, seize fanatically upon one heritage to the exclusion of the other,
denying themselves of much on which they could feed.

Fortunately, there is an inexorable and continuing interplay between
our native and other heritages, modifying and refining it without destroying
its essence—in music, architecture, literature, and mindset. These verses
record some of my own such experiences with other heritages: the Puerto
Rico of my boyhood, adequately expressed only in the unusually musical lan-
guage of that world, Spanish; and, later, another world, Romanian, with new
insights, different perceptions, and new ways of thinking—the world of
Eliade, Brancusi, Enesco, Ionesco, Tzara, Celan, and Cioran—the world that
intrigued even the Hungarian and Transylvanian composer Bartok in his
later years; a world ever conscious of its roots in an autochthonous past, in
the Carpathian forests (its home for generations), in its sense of symbiosis
with the land—a people with a multiplaned consciousness, always aware of
both the immediate and the timeless, the temporal and the transcendental,
the abstract and the concrete.

These poems also show an awareness of the challenges today to reli-
gious faith and seek to reconcile our religious heritage with those chal-
lenges—to assimilate the vistas of science into that faith.

Though my youthful attempts at versifying concentrated on such rigid
forms as the sonnet, ballad, sestina, and villanelle, these poems are in free
verse or metered verse without end rhymes, allowing me the freedom to
be more exact in a choice of words that would best convey my meanings
by relying on overtones and the special rhythms of internal rhymes, asso-
nances, and alliterations, on euphony and cadence and sometimes meter, to
maintain musicality and heighten feeling. I have avoided the free association
of much of modern verse, preferring instead the more direct approach of
older poetry, while keeping the music of words and phrases.

—Thomas Amherst Perry

WHERE, THEN, IS THE SUN?

I.

FROM THESE ROOTS

The branching tree sends forth its roots,
Drawing life from the rich and ageless loam,
Always with ample space to grow and change,
But always deeply rooted in that loam.
From these roots it seeks the distant sun.

Man has roots too,
Deep into rich loam stored with nutrients
Tried and wisely winnowed by the years.
He, too, must grow and change,
But always fed from that store in the ageless soil.
From these roots he, too, can seek the sun.

O BRAVE NEW WORLD

T' whom Satan turning boldly: Chaos and ancient
Night, I come, . . . that Region lost, . . . [to] reduce her
original darkness and your sway.
>—Milton, *Paradise Lost*

We shall proclaim destruction. . . . [W]e'll spread
a few legends. . . . And the whole earth will resound with
the cry: "A new and righteous law is coming."
>—Dostoevsky, *The Devils*

[T]his impulse of mankind toward self-destruction
and Nothingness, specifically its manifestation in the
sphere of organizing society.
>—Igor Shafarevich, *The Socialist Phenomenon*

Night beckons, relentlessly:
Come back.
Come back.
Come back to the void!
Back to the formless.
Back to Nothingness.
Come, Fenrir, son of Loki!
Come, Ancient Chaos!

God is dead, and His Creation is no more.
No more His laws.
Shed our heritage, uproot our past.
Now we shape a new, more modern world,
Up to date, in keeping with the times.
One that better fits our fancy.

Now the siren song
For a brave new world where
Liberty serves desire.
Where we shout with Caliban,

O freedom, freedom, heyday freedom!
Now Gonzalo's golden age
(No magistrates, perfection)
Where we can execute all things.
Replace old Mother Nature
With more permissive canon.
Where we divorce effect from cause,
Deny the consequence.
Decide what is right and what is wrong
By the polls, by majority vote.
Replace our heritage with myths that better serve the
Cause.
Where we raise altars to the flesh,
Eat, drink, and are merry—
Then die . . .

Back,
Back.
Back to the deep dark void,
Back to the primal pit,
Back to nothingness.

O brave new world!

JESUS ON THE MOUNT OF TEMPTATION

Jesus stood on the mountain top, John and the Jordan far below,
And the Voice, "Thou art the Messiah!"
Below, the city of the David, who made a kingdom.
Below the city of Pilate, the deputy of Rome, a greater kingdom.
To the south below, the land of Egypt;
To the east the Petraean hills; northward, Syria.
All around, the realm of Caesar,
The great and mighty, empowered Caesar.

At Jesus's side appeared the Devil.
The Devil waved to all these kingdoms,
And the Devil said to Jesus,
"You are the Messiah. This World can be yours.
To bring your kingdom here on Earth,
You need a State, like Caesar's.
You must lead a social revolution.
You must legislate and regulate to have your Paradise.
All that men have and all that men can get
Must belong to a State, so you can say what each can keep,
So you can mete and dole as you deem fit and just,
So you can force compassion and good will.
With laws and regulations you can right all wrongs, cure all ills.
The State would be Father to the People.
And you would have your Kingdom here on Earth."

But Jesus said, "Get thee hence. The Lord God is Father.
His kingdom, my kingdom, is not of this world:
The kingdom of God is within, not without.
In the kingdom of my father,
The righteous, fired by His Spirit,

Feel compassion and good will,
Feed the hungry, give drink to the thirsty,
Take in the stranger, clothe the naked,
Visit those who are sick, come unto those in prison,
Even to the least of these.
Like good seed, the Kingdom will spring and bring forth fruit.
Like a grain of mustard, the least of all the seeds
That when grown is the greatest among the herbs
And becomes a mighty tree, the kingdom will spread its branches.
Like the leaven hid in measures of meal it will leaven the whole.
God's kingdom is light that will spread through darkness."
Jesus said, "This is my kingdom. Begone!"

The Devil shrugged his shoulders: "Oh, well, there's always a Barabas."
And the Devil departed.

Jesus came down—
Not to the rebels of Zion, not to the politics of Rome—
But down to hearts and minds—
In Galilee.

MUST I BE A RACE?

(According to a recent news story, a young woman filling out an application to a college protested being required to choose between a Black and a White parent in identifying "her race.")

Must I be a race? Pigeonholed?
Must you color me white or black?
Brown or red or yellow?
Everywhere "Race? Check one:
Caucasian □ Afro □ Hispanic □
Native American □ Asian □."

Which one? My father a porter on the Santa Fe,
My mother an Anglo-Saxon maid.
Mine the heritage
From Washington Carver and Abraham Lincoln.

Which one? My father a don of Santa Fe,
My mother a Boston blueblood.
Mine the heritage
From Emerson and Coronado.

Which one? My father a Scotch-Irish farmhand,
My mother a Californian Nisei.
Mine the heritage
From Woodrow Wilson and the Emperor of Japan.

Which one? My father a Cherokee,
My mother a British schoolmarm.
Mine the heritage
From Sequoyah and Winston Churchill.

Which one? My father a Negro ranchhand,
My mother a Texas señorita.
Mine the heritage
From Luther King and Benito Juarez.

Which one? My father, a red-haired Celt,
My mother a yellow octaroon—
One eighth Afro, seven eighths white—
Which race am I?

Which one. My father the darkest Black,
My mother a brown mulatto—
One fourth white, three fourths Afro—
Which race am I?

Which one? My grandmother, Puertorican,
My grandfather, an immigrant Pole.
My other grandmother a Cajun maid,
The grandsire a Choctaw soldier boy.
In this melting pot of genes,
Which race am I?

Label us not: We have roots in more than one soil.

Note:
    "[T]he country is entering a new era in which old racial categories are rapidly becoming obsolete ... The rapid increase in mixed-race children means that, in the not-too-distant future, it will be virtually impossible to sort Americans into precise categories . . . [B]y ending racial classification . . . Americans can take an important step toward transcending the historic barriers of race . . . [But] against their better instincts, young people are being corrupted into thinking of themselves in racial terms and into developing identities and hostilities that will only prove a barrier into further reducing the vestiges of racism in America."—Dinesh D'Souza, *The End of Racism*, with permission.

OFFERTORY

All things come of thee, O Mighty State,
All that we have is thine, and thine alone,
And of thine own do we give back to thee.

II.

THE UNSEEN

[T]he material world we inhabit is but a shadowy likeness of a transcendent world . . . that is timeless and perfect, like the world of Plato.
—Roger Penrose, British mathematical physicist, as quoted in a *Wall Street Journal* review of his *Shadows of the Mind* (January 9, 1995)

I.

Early Man felt the Unseen
And peopled it with daemons.

Greek and Roman felt the Unseen,
And peopled it with nymphs and fauns.

The Celt felt the Unseen,
And peopled it with faeries and leprechauns.

II.

Science probed the Unseen,
And found a universe of cosmic rays and dancing quarks.

Physics probed the Unseen,
And found deep black holes, with universes warping time and space.

III.

Plato found in the Unseen a creator Logos
Revealing itself in shadows of the mind.

The Poet found in the Unseen an unseen Presence
Interfused in ocean, sun, and the mind of Man.

The Oxford don found in mathematics
A transcendent, timeless, Platonic world of forms.

IV.

There are more things in this world, Horatio,
Than are dreamed of in your philosophy.

—Revised from *Songs on the Wind*, National Library of Poetry, 1995

I AM

Who am I?
You call me Brahma.
You call me Theos.
You call me Manitou.
You call me El, Yahweh, Allah.
You call me Deus, Dios, Dieu.
You call me Bog, Dumnezeu.
You call me Gott, God.

What am I?
You say I am king, I am lord.
You say I am Father, Mother.
You say I am the Almighty, the Creator.
You say I am the Demiurge.
You say I am First Cause, the Primum Mobile, the Life Force.
You say I am Providence.
You say I am the Logos.
You say I am Truth.

12

Who am I?
What am I?
I am Spirit, but you are flesh
And can no more
Than see through a glass darkly.

So I say simply:
I AM.

GENESIS

In the beginning?

In the beginning a Mind.
In the beginning a Logos*.
In the beginning, God.
In the beginning God created the heavens and the earth.
In the beginning a Mind programmed this world.
In the beginning the Logos was with God, and the Logos was God,
All things were made by him and without him was not anything made.

In the beginning there was no form, only a void,
And darkness was upon the deep.
The spirit of God moved upon the face of the deep,
And there was a flash of energy and light,
An electric dance with frenzied, darting particles.
Waves of photons sped across the space.

And it was the morning and the evening ** of the first day.***
It was the beginning and the end of the first great Age.

14

God said, Let there be a firmament, and there was space.
Within the space He cooled the fiery storm, slowed the frantic dance.
From the deaths of clashing quanta He brought forth matter.
From the matter He programmed building blocks:
Atoms, molecules, elements.
He gathered the elements together
Into wheeling clouds, into galaxies.

It was the morning and the evening of the second day.
It was the beginning and the end of the second great Age.

Within the galaxies God shaped huge clumps of matter:
Suns and stars, moons and planets—and Earth.
And on them He placed crusts of land.
On Earth the clouds dissolved to waters.
God gathered the waters into seas and lakes and rivers.

It was the morning and the evening of the third day.
It was the beginning and the end of the third great Age.

God said, On Earth let there be life, in the seas, one-celled living plants.
He programmed genes in them that they might multiply,
Each after its own kind.
Then He molded multi-celled plants:
Algae—green and blue and brown and red—
And the long-stemmed giant kelp.

God said, In the seas let there be animals,
Microscopic one-celled animals: amoeba, paramecia.
He molded multi-celled animals: sponges, worms, and jellyfish.
Then He made the turtles, the snakes, the fish, and finally the great sea mammals.
He programmed genes in them that they might multiply,
Each after its own kind.

The waters brought forth these living creatures abundantly.

It was the morning and the evening of the fourth day.
It was the beginning and the end of the fourth great Age.

God said, Let the land bring forth life.
Seaweed washed ashore, spawned fungi, mosses, ferns.
He seeded reeds in swamps, grass upon dry land.
He made the herbs, the tall, green pines, the leafing trees, the multicolored flowers.

God said, Let the land also bring forth animals, creeping things.
Sea creatures crawled ashore.
God made the scorpions, then the dinosaurs and lizards.
Finally, He made the cattle and the beasts.
He made the fowls that fly above the earth in the open sky.
In all of these he programmed genes that they might multiply,
Each after its own kind.

This was the morning and the evening of the fifth day.
It was the beginning and the end of the fifth great Age.

God said, Let us make Man in Our Image, after Our likeness.
He made Man in His own Image,
With Mind,
And Will,
And Heart.
He let Man know what is good,
And what is evil,
With the freedom to choose.

Male and female, God created them.
He said, Be fruitful and multiply,
Replenish the earth.
Have dominion over it,
And partners with Him, create.

And Man became a living Soul.

This was the morning and the evening of the sixth day.
This was the beginning and the end of the sixth great Age.

God paused and looked at all that He had made:
Into the void, order—
Into the dark, light.
Into the deep, energy and movement:
A vast electric universe
With spinning spheres tuned to ordered paths.

Into barrenness,
The vibrancy and growth of life.

Among the beasts,
An image of Himself,
Man.

Then God said,
Behold it is good.
It is very, very good.

* logos: (Greek: word, reason, plan) "The divine reason implicit in the cosmos,
ordering it and giving it form and meaning"
—*Encyclopedia Britannica.* Also see John 1:1-3.

** morning: "The beginning or early part of anything likened to a day."
—*Oxford Dictionary*

** evening: "The closing or declining period of anything compared to a day."
—*Oxford Dictionary*

*** day: "The time during which anything exists or takes place, time, era."
—*Oxford Dictionary*

MESSAGE FROM VOYAGER

Not a smidgeon.
   —Monitor of the last message from Voyager when asked if there had
                              been any evidence of life in outer space.

Not a smidgeon.
Not a smidgeon!
No life anywhere!

The learned astronomer shook his head
As he studied the *Voyager* log . . .
Then stared into the dark, into dead and barren space.

No green, green grass,
No amber fields of grain,
No scented blooms,
No leafing trees,

No darting fish,
No soaring eagle,
No whippoorwill,
No frisky colt,
No playful pup,
No breathing, thinking Man—
Anywhere out there.

Alone.
All all alone within a vast and awesome space.
Just us and the Creator in this vast and awesome space.

                              —From *Dark Side of the Moon*
          (Editor's Choice Award National Library of Poetry, 1994)

JOURNEY INTO SPACE—AND TIME

We might be seeing our own origins in all of this but also of the entire cosmos.
—Robert Williams
Director of the Hubbell Observatory.

This beautiful picture is seeing galaxies in the process of forming [the first stage in the lumping of matter into galaxies] ... Some ... of the images ... are the first galaxies.
—Craig Hogan
Cosmologist at the University of Washington after viewing the pictures relayed by the Hubbell telescope December 1995 when it focused on the outer limits of space, as quoted in the January 29, 1996, issue of *Newsweek*

After the Avis of Portugal
Winged into the untried Western seas
And the Genoan in the Santa Maria
Sailed into the fearsome Western space,
Followed by the curious: Cabot, Hudson,
Vespucci and Magellan,
Slowly piercing the Unknown;
After the unveiling of the Western seas—

The Danish Tycho and the Paduan
Looked upwards into other Spaces,
And with a new found Eye
Began a journey into this other Space—and Time.
The Moon disclosed its craters,
And a new world appeared,
A family of suns and sibling planets,
Our native galaxy.

Others, curious too,
Slowly probed this new and fearsome space:
Kepler with his formulae,
Gilbert and Newton,

With travel into space, travel back in time.
Hubbell ventured beyond our galaxy,
Hawking and Penrose found
The primordial exotic particles
And the cosmos eons ago.

Today we stare at the edge of infinity.

Will some great Eye next capture images
Of speeding photons in the Big Bang?
Back into the beginning of time?

TRANSLATION

When I was thrust into this strange and awesome world,
I gave myself to What was here,
In trust to caring arms.

When I leave,
I shall slip into another strange and awesome world
And give myself to What is there,
Entrust myself to other caring arms.

ROOTS
IN OTHER
SOILS

1. BAYAMÓN, PUERTO RICO (1919-1927)

2. ROMANIA (1963-64, 1968, 1972, 1978)

SONIDOS BORINQUEÑOS

En la noche,
En la noche,
Sonidos borinqueños.

El *coquí, coquí*
De las ranillas
En el mango sombreando nuestra casa.

El *shik-a-shik, shik-a-shik*
Del güiro
Del baile
En el barrio
A través la vega.

La dulce picadura
Del mandolina
Y apasionada canto
Del novio
Serenando
La bella vecina.

El *bum . . . bum*
De las ollas
Del invisible mar.

En las vacaciones estivales
En las montañas de Dajaos
El resonante canto
Del ciego aguador
Bajando por la vereda
Hasta el río—
Su décima jíbara
Reverberando entre las colinas.

Los sonidos,
Los sonidos,
En la noche borinqueña.

Borinquen is the Indian, and poetic name for Puerto Rico.
The coquí is the small tree frog.
The güiro is a Puertorican musical instrument made from a gourd to provide the
dance rhythm.

—From Touchstone, 17 (1992)

DOÑA MARÍA

Doña María: arroz, habichuelas, y ajo,
Garbanzos, bacalao,
Guineos fritos, aguacates sabrosos.

Doña María: camisas almidonadas,
Sabanas blanqueadas con sol borinqueño,
Jabón Octagon.

Doña María: leyendas boricuas,
Triunfos del pícaro Juan Bobo,
Cuentos del vudú en Haiti.

Doña María: la violencia de San Ciriaco,
Techos y palmas volando,
Aguas del río hasta su choza en el barrio.

Doña María: borinqueña,
Cara arrugada y morena,
Materna y cariñosa.

Doña María, mi hermana, y yo.

arroz, habichuelas, ajo: rice and beans with garlic
bacalao: codfish
guineos fritos: fried bananas
aguacates. avocados
borinqueña: Puertorican
boricua: Puertorican
San Ciriaco: the hurricane of 1899
choza: shanty

—From *Touchstone*, 19 (1994)

NAVIDAD PUERTORIQUEÑA

O santícisimo, felicísimo,
Grato tiempo de Navidad . . .
*Alegría, alegría, Cristiandad.**

El Día de los Inocentes
Con sus burlas y diablitos vestidos de rojo.
La noche de la natividad con sus villancicos,
Sus pesebres y la Virgen María.

El Día de los Reyes:**
De noche las cajitas con yerba,
Y el vaso de agua al lado de los lechos,
Para los magos y sus caballos.

Los Magos vinieron a Belén,
Para anunciar la venida del Mesías,
Nosotros con alegría,
*Lo anunciamos hoy tambien.****

De manaña, llenas las calles con niños,
Con sus gritos jubilosos,
Muchachos con pitos y pelotas,
Niñas acarisiando sus muñecas.

Alegría, alegría!
Felicísimo, grato tiempo de Navidad!
. . . .

* Christmas hymn.
** Twelfth Night, Three Kings Day
*** Puertorican carol.

Note:
   Santa Claus passes up the Puertorican child, but on Twelfth Night (January 6) he can expect a visit from the Three Wise Men, who bring him gifts—not down a chimney (there are none in Puerto Rico, anyway)—but through the door. Grass in a little box and a cup of water beside the bed, for the horses (or camels), await the visitors.

Down the street from our home in Bayamón, Puerto Rico (at that time a small city of about twelve thousand population), was the town home of Virgilio Dávila, one of the island's major poets and a gentleman farmer. Besides more sophisticated poems, he also wrote—with the composer Don Braulio Dueño, also my violin teacher—several songs for school children, some of which I knew by heart and often sang. His other poems showed a love and sympathy for small town people and for animal life, with flashes of humor and a nostalgia for the simple life. He was especially fond of the sonnet form, and published a series of them. His sonnet, "The Ox," is a favorite of mine and also recalls the many times oxen pulled carts of sugar cane down the street in front of our house.

THE OX

The bullock bends to the yoke, to toil
Submissive at the cart, strains
To plow the clay-hard stubborn soil,
Never rebels, never complains.

Within the furrows he pitilessly trudges,
Endures the prod, slogs along,
Plods his weary way and drudges,
Will not curse like the butchered hog.

He is a dead one since that fateful day
When taken from his herd, away
To serve the will of tyrant Man.

Sometimes he gives a mournful bellow,
Because the bullock has a soul—
Illusions shattered in alien land.

—Virgilio Dávila (1869-1943), "El Buey." Copyright held by Editorial Cordillera. Translated by Thomas Amherst Perry, with permission.

Sometimes we would spend part of our summer vacation in the mountains of Dajaos, south of Bayamón. Often in the evening as we sat on the front porch, a blind water carrier would come down the mountain path quite a distance away, a yoke with water jugs across his shoulders and singing a folk song that echoed across the valley. His vibrant voice still rings in my memory. It could have been a décima like the following, a folk song form brought to Puerto Rico by Andalusians from Spain, many of them ancestors of the jíbaros who settled in the mountains of this island. It consisted of a ten-line stanza of eight-syllable lines, and was divided into two quintillas, two sections of five lines each. The rhyme scheme was aabba ccddc. It became the most popular verse form among the common people.

DÉCIMA: HOW SAD THE COOING OF A DOVE

How sad the cooing of a dove
In the dusk of a wooded grove.
Sad, a woman with lover gone
Pacing an endless night alone,
Yearning for him who is her love.

But he has yet to serve a year,
One long year, heavy weight to bear.
And she cannot last it out, though
It is but sadder still to know
A betrayal by one so dear.

—Folk song from the Dajaos region, "Qué triste es una paloma," recorded by F. Manrique Cabrera. Translated by Thomas Amherst Perry.

Selection from S O N G   O F   T H E   B A M B O O

Mysterious song of the bamboo,
Intoned for its capricious friend, the breeze.

. . . . . .

The buxom, fresh morning
Dons the first of her garments.
No sooner is she dressed than I waken
And listen to the bamboo's strange, enigmatic song,
With its whispers of kisses and sighs, of poems,
Brought from who knows where and from what distance
On the wings of the breeze.

As the day deepens
With its growing light and emerging colors,
The song becomes rhythmic and gentle, languid, deliberate.
The dragon fly settles,
Rests its small body of bright lustrous gauze
On the leaves of the bamboo tree.
It departs, returns.
It may know that strange, enigmatic song of the bamboo tree.

The butterflies—flowers in flight—
Draw near, and frolicking, play through the branches,
While the lighthearted linnet warbles a harmony.
It has nested there,
Perhaps to learn this mysterious ballad,
Which the bamboo sings for its friend, the capricious breeze.

When evening gathers her tunic,
Resplendent and golden, around the bamboo,
When the libellula hides, fearful, in the branches—
When the butterflies sleep, and the linnet is silent,

The song of the bamboo turns sad—slow, murmursome, placid.
Its fronds bend down,
Its leaves are like the shivering tears of a clouded emerald.

. . . . .

The Bamboo now sings more softly,
More slowly, more murmursome,
More placid than ever.
Its fronds lean over.
And the song ends.

—Concepción Meléndez, "La Canción del Bambú." Copyright by Editura
Cordillera. Translated by Thomas Amherst Perry, with permission.

My arrival in Romania in 1963 coincided with dramatic changes in that country. My appointment to the University of Bucharest was but one aspect of the Cultural Exchange which marked a partial thaw in the relations of our countries, partly after the death of Stalin, but accelerated now, and marked by an amnesty for many writers and intellectuals heretofore blacklisted but now rehabilitated. I soon became aware of the revival of a Romanian mindset and discovered an expression of it in the poet Tudor Arghezi, still alive and now the subject of study by a young British exchange student, Michael Impey, soon to become my friend. Like others of his generation in the Golden Age (1920-1940), Arghezi looked to the ancient Romanian past and identified himself with its long history, often painful and servile, rooted for centuries in the Carpathian soil. His "Testament" (1927), probably his most popular poem, now resurrected, shows this mindset. Significantly he uses the form of the old Romanian folk verse—couplets in a meter similar to our tetrameters.

Selection from T E S T A M E N T

I leave no goods to you when I am dead,
Just my name upon a book instead.
In the rebel evening coming through
From my forefathers down to you,
Over cliffs, down ravines,
Which our ancestors climbed on hands and knees,

. . . .

I bring this book.
Place it at the head of your bed,
A legacy, the first you have had
From the serfs in sheepskin coats to thee,
Serfs, whose bones now rest in me.

. . . .

The tongue with which they called their herds
Now is woven into fitting words.

. . . .

All the people's grief and pain
I have built into a violin.

. . . .
The ashes of people dead and gone
I have shaped into a god of stone.
. . . .
[And] . . . buried deep within
Simmers the wrath of my ancient kin.

—Tudor Arghezi (1880-1967), "Testament." Selection translated by Thomas
Amherst Perry.

PSALM: LORD, DO YOU HEAR?

Lord, do you hear?

"Put your hand against your breast, Son, and listen with the
palm of your hand."

God walks by.
His footstep is gentle. He treads as if on wings.
His touch is like a feather.

I ask, "Is it you, Lord?"
And he answers, "I am here."

—Tudor Arghezi, "Dumnezeu, îl auzi?" Translated by Thomas Amherst Perry.

Selection from PSALM: GIVE ME, O LORD, KNOWLEDGE

Give me, O Lord,
Knowledge to understand Thee,
For I have no notion of
How I may become aware of Thee.
My mind cannot scrutinize Thee.
My senses cannot comprehend Thee.
I cannot see or hear you.
You lie beyond the bounds of my senses.

—Tudor Arghezi, "Dă-mi, Doamne, stiinta." Translated by Thomas
Amherst Perry.

PSALM: A MADMAN DUG DEEPLY

A madman dug deeply into a mound to seek a hoard of silver,
And dug feverishly until nightfall.
He dug the whole night through until daylight filled the hole.
When nightfall came again, he began his labors again.
At daybreak he found nothing. His arms were numb with weariness.

What strange creature would labor in vain in such a forbidden spot?
It is I, Lord. I seek you, who created the world and knows my labor is
in vain.

    —Tudor Arghezi, "Un nebun a înfipt lopata." Translated by Thomas
Amherst Perry.

Note:
    Throughout his life Arghezi was beset by a spiritual restlessness, from time
to time expressed in a cry for spiritual reassurance, most evident in his Psalms.
Early entering the orthodox priesthood as a monk, he next found himself pur-
suing theological studies at a Roman Catholic monastery near Fribourg,
Switzerland. He soon abandoned monasticism, dissatisfied with religious dogma,
but at times independently sought contact with the Divine, a lonely soul fright-
ened by the prospect of a cosmos without certainty. Although finally accepting
a chaotic demiurgic universe, he periodically returned to his search, often pre-
occupied with questions about death.

Some time later I became acquainted with another aspect of the Romanian mindset: its multiplaned perception of reality. As Mircea Eliade (whom I had the privilege of meeting a few years later and talking to about this mindset) has observed, in the Romanian mind "there is a camouflage of the fantastic in the daily event," a play between the concrete and the abstract, between the timeless and the immediate.

I found this especially in the verse of the poet Ion Barbu, who had died two years before, in 1961. In "Dioptric," a reader peers through his spectacles at a medieval book with its ornate letters. The poet makes uses of the double meanings of "prism" (the spectacles and the mental processes of getting meaning from the book), "saturation of a sign" (meaning from print), "foliate" and "leaf vibrating like a drum" (leaves decorating the letters, the leafs of the book, the mental excitement in reading). There are the two planes of reality in the "gossamer dream," the learned "tome," the litter, and the cleaning women. In "Counter Play," there are two planes: a world perceived by the poet and the temporal world, symbolized by two counter worlds, one above and one below a water surface, and by two worlds on opposite sides of a mirror. The temporal world does not know the hidden reality which the poet perceives.

DIOPTRIC

From high on the spectrum, prisms ponder
The saturation of a sign, foliate.
Like choice wine, the caulicoles redden,
Though the sun sets at the rim in mourning crape.

Nearer, the eyes squint fixedly
At the leaf vibrating like a drum,
At the crown of the letter, bramble-like,
Heavy in the low flutter from the hearth.

The chamber curves in a gossamer dream!
Next day, tidied up by old women, it passes by,
And litter is shaped into cones, immured in tomes.
From embers the coming of a day.

—Ion Barbu (1895-1961), "Dioptrie." From *Paintbrush*, 1977. Copyright held by Ishtar Press. Translated by Thomas Amherst Perry, with permission.

COUNTER PLAY

Inferred, in the deep beneath this calm crest,
As if thrust through a mirror into a freed empyrean,
Cutting through the drowning country herd
In swirls of water, is a shadow world, a purer dance.

Oh latent nadir! The poet raises up the sum
Of scattered harps lost in that inverted flight.
And a hidden song pours forth, like the sea
Swaying jellyfish as they stroll under verdant bells.

—Ion Barbu from, "Joc Secund." From *Contemporary East European Poetry* (Ardis, 1983, Oxford University Press, 1993). Translated by Thomas Amherst Perry.

ABOUT THE AUTHOR

Thomas Amherst Perry, native of Nebraska, lived his boyhood years in Puerto Rico, where his parents, the Rev. Thomas Charles and Mable Avis Perry, were missionaries under the United Christian Missionary Society. A graduate of the State Preparatory School of Colorado and Park College, he received the Ph.D. degree in English from the University of Iowa and later studied at the International Summer School at Oxford University.

A college teacher of English, he has held full time faculty positions at Park College, the University of Iowa, Central Methodist College (department head), Southwestern University (Texas), and East Texas State University, now Texas A & M University-Commerce, (department head and Professor Emeritus); and served as visiting Professor of English at Northeast Missouri State College, the University of Missouri at Columbia, and, under the Smith-Mundt Act, at the Universidad Autónoma del Estado de México. He was the first Fulbright Lecturer in American Language and Literature at the University of Bucharest in Romania, and revisited Romania under research grants. He is a recognized Shakespeare and Renaissance scholar and authority on aspects of Romanian literature, and has been listed in the *Directory of American Scholars*, *Who's Who in the Midwest*, and *Who's Who in the South and Southwest*. His poems, original and translations, have appeared in literary magazines and anthologies. He was honored with the Distinguished Faculty Award at East Texas State University and the Distinguished Alumnus Award from Park College. In 1981 he was elected to full membership in the American Romanian Academy of Arts and Sciences.

He currently resides with his wife, Lora Margaret, in Commerce, Texas. They are the parents of four children: Laura Massie, administrative librarian; Dr. Robert Thomas Perry, university administrator; Dr. Timothy T. Perry, university professor; and Charles Lee Perry, lawyer.